Reviews for *The Gift of Courage*

"In 28 years in the sales field, I've had an opportunity to experience volumes of articles and books on motivation and inspiration. None compares to the unique, tender, moving approach to that subject than *The Gift of Courage*. Read it often!"

John M. Delich, President
Mutual of Omaha Funds

"*The Gift of Courage* is the cornerstone of my professional library. It is a must for every person who wants to achieve above-average performance. It provides the necessary motivation to turn down days into successful ventures."

Paul A. Smihal, CPA
Director of State & Local Taxes
Coopers & Lybrand

"What a wonderful little classic *The Gift of Courage* is! Truly a book after my own heart. I have always lived by its principles, and have tried fervently to inspire such courage in others—particularly people who want to write. This powerful yet charming book would have helped me; I wish I'd had it long ago."

Marjorie Holmes
America's favorite
inspirational writer,
as described by
The New York Times

"Courage is difficult to define. But with faith in God all things are possible and this is the bottom line of courage."

Karl Kassulke
Former Minnesota Viking
National Football League

The Gift of Courage

The Gift of Courage

Paul Speicher
Foreword by Hugh P. O'Kane

DICTION BOOKS
1313 Fifth Street S.E., Suite 104B
Minneapolis, MN 55414

A Gift Within Your Grasp

Copyright © 1956, 1986 by Diction Books
First published in 1956 by
Research & Review Service of America, Inc./R&R Newkirk Publication
Reprint edition 1986 by Diction Books

ISBN: 0-9609198-3-X

Library of Congress Catalog Card Number: 84-073533

All rights reserved. No part of this publication nor any of its related products may be reproduced or transmitted in any form or by any means, electronic or mechanical, including photocopying, recording, or by any information storage and retrieval system, without written permission from Diction Books.

Foreword

Early in my career of selling I realized that motivation was one of the very special tools needed for my life's work. I had learned the principles and mechanics involved in selling. I had attended countless seminars and had been involved in hundreds of conversations with people from all walks of life. However, I found that theory without motivation was ultimately useless. My quest was that one ingredient needed to spur me on to success—to learn what separated the average from the superior.

My life was transformed when I was first given a copy of this book, *The Gift of Courage*. It gave me the dogged determination to act now, the motivation to keep on trying, and most especially it gave me the courage to utilize my full potential. I memorized its pages and recited them in my car enroute to sales calls. Because of that practice, I found myself able to do what all my mentors had ceaselessly preached—to tell my story with feeling and enthusiasm.

What can I say about Paul Speicher, author of this book? He is a man whom I never met, but whose writings have been a part of my daily life for over 28 years. I can and do say that he has my heartfelt gratitude. Quite possibly, without the inspiration of this man's writings, I would now find myself in the meadow with the sheep rather than on the hillside with the lions.

My relationship with God and the need to get on my knees daily to converse with Him goes without saying. He is my first priority. *The Gift of Courage* will never replace that part of my life—nor should it in your life. However, with my faith sustaining me on a spiritual level and this book motivating me on a personal level, I have achieved more than I had ever hoped or dared.

I challenge you to accept the gift of courage and welcome its message into your life. I will look for you on the hillside with the lions.

Hugh P. O'Kane
Vice President and Senior Partner
Juran & Moody, Incorporated

Whether you be man or woman you will never do anything without courage. It is the greatest quality of the mind next to honor.

—JAMES L. ALLEN

Contents

Foreword	*i*
The Gift of Courage	1
Chapter I *The Courage to Act Now*	3
Chapter II *The Courage to Keep on Trying*	5
Chapter III *The Lifting Power and Reward of Courage*	7
Chapter IV *The Courage to Meet Life's Daily Tests*	9
Chapter V *The Courage to Keep Your Mind Free From Worry*	11
Chapter VI *The Courage that Comes From Constructive Thinking*	13
Chapter VII *The Courage to Utilize Your Full Potential*	15
Chapter VIII *The Courage to Meet Mental Depressions*	19
Chapter IX *The Courage of Dogged Determination*	23
Chapter X *The Kind of Courage Needed*	25
The Priceless Jewel	31
Recommended Reading	33
Index	35
About the Author	37
Why This Book Was Reprinted	39

The Gift of Courage

The Gift of Courage

If you could have as a gift your dearest wish fulfilled, the wish that lies closest to your heart, the thing that you want most in the world, what would you choose?

A million dollars? Abounding health? A magic solution to business worries? A contented mind? A devoted family? The privilege of traveling only on the hill-tops in the morning sun? Escape from the ills of life which are common to all?

What gift would be more worthy of you than the fulfillment of an idle day dream? What one thing would help you win through the problems you face today and may face again tomorrow? What gift would enable you to enjoy because you have fought, to rest because you have labored, to reap because you have sown?

> *There is such a gift within your grasp, a gift which you yourself can give yourself, a gift which will bring all the things for which you secretly long, a gift which like magic will help clear the troubled roadway ahead and set your feet upon the pathway to real happiness.*
>
> *And that gift is the Gift of Courage.*

Greater than intellect, experience, ability, foresight is the fighting edge that is his when a man is not afraid of the future, when with self-confidence he heeds the call to each day's struggle, and when he crashes into that struggle with a drive that comes only when heart, mind and body are flooded with courage.

The gift of courage is the greatest gift you can give yourself!

I

The Courage to Act Now

Give yourself the courage to crash into each day's problems and do the things today that have to be done. The curse of life is procrastination, under the spell of which some men sit and wait for fairer days, wasting life as they wait, while its beads slip unchecked through listless fingers.

Life wastes them while they waste life.

Ulysses tells us of the land of the lotus eaters in which men dwelt, forgetting home and family and native land, wandering about sad-eyed, dreaming dreams that never could come true. There is another land, the land of Pretty-Soon which is as dangerous to human hopes as the fabled land of the lotus. The road that leads to that mystic land is strewn with pitiful wrecks, and the ships that have sailed for its shining strands bear skeletons on their decks; it is farther at noon than it was at dawn and farther at night than at noon.

O. Henry tells the story of the New York artist who planned a great masterpiece. His picture was to be colossal. Those who heard him tell his plans were thrilled by the conception. It would send his name echoing forever down the ageless corridors of time. It would make of him a companion of the immortal da Vinci, the magnificent Rembrandt.

But he couldn't start the picture today. Things weren't right. A touch of rheumatism. A gloomy day. Bad light. So it went, until one day his friends found him dead in bed. They took up his lifeless body and buried his masterpiece with him.

> *Will the masterpiece you have hoped to make of life be buried with you? Someday you are going to set a record. Someday you are going to do things that will surprise everyone. Someday you are going to startle the world with your accomplishments. Someday you are going to lick forever the troublesome problems that worry you. Someday you are going to get tired of standing outside, and you are going to force your way into life's banquet hall and demand your place at the table. Someday.*

But while you talk about someday, the days slip away, the fabric of life grows thin, and many a man dies with his masterpiece unpainted, his dreams buried with him.

Give yourself the courage today to make the first step toward the things you have been talking for years about doing. A great gift it is for it will enable you to act before the years have fled and taken with them the glory you had hoped to find in life.

The Courage to Keep on Trying

Give yourself the courage to keep on trying. Have we ever any right to stamp failure on our foreheads?

When is a man a failure? Is he a failure when his business falls off? Is he a failure when he determines upon a goal and fails to make it? Is he a failure when a month goes by and he has had no success? Is he a failure when he is discouraged?

No! Disheartening as these things are, they do not make him a failure.

A man is a failure when he has quit trying. Then and only then. Write that truth deep in your heart and come back to it time and time again.

Booth Tarkington wrote short stories for five years before a single story was accepted. If he had stopped during those distressing years, Tarkington would have been a failure. But so long as he did not stop, so long as he kept on writing stories and sending them to publishers, he was not a failure.

Robert Louis Stevenson's first book was condemned so heartlessly by the critics that Stevenson contemplated suicide. But instead of committing suicide, he wrote another book and another and still another, until at last the literary world knelt in admiration at his feet. If he had stopped trying, Stevenson would have been a failure.

If you could look into the inner life of almost any successful man you would find long months and long years when nothing that he did seemed to bring results. You would find him time and again despairing of achievement, and yet you would find him working on doggedly through his despair.

Had he stopped trying, he would have been a failure. But he didn't stop trying.

To him who endureth shall come the victory.

A man is a failure only when he quits trying.

The Lifting Power and Reward of Courage

More men deprive the world of their talents by lacking the courage to go into action than by all other means. Many men go to their graves unsung for want of a little more courage! They sit and sit. They think and think. They plan and plan. But they never muster the courage to act.

The lifting power of courage is so great that overnight it can change your whole life. Courage sends problems and obstacles spinning into oblivion. Granted integrity and intelligence, most men need only added courage to rise to the stars. Man and courage, what an unbeatable combination!

Let me repeat—the lifting power of courage is so great that it can change your whole life!

So in your prayers tonight, pray also for courage.

Give yourself the courage to believe that rewards will surely come.

Impatience is a common fault, which leads us into all sorts of mental upsets, and spoils many an otherwise good day. Occasionally we may make a little spurt of effort. Instead of taking a nap on Sunday afternoon, we work for an hour at the office. We work late three or four nights in a row. We push ourselves hard for three or four weeks, and then we lean back with a self-righteous air and wonder why life does not richly reward our extra effort. We have the nervous impatience of a child, and often we howl if we can't have our extra profits right here and now.

Of course it takes courage to be patient and to keep on going on at top speed when extra rewards are not immediately forthcoming. But patient we must be.

Remember how Ben Hur stood up under the lash of the galley master, bending to the oars as heartily as if he were on a pleasure cruise, eagerly changing from one side to the other of the boat in order that his body might develop uniformly.

Ben Hur might have said each night, "Of what avail is the struggle, or wherein does the effort profit? I am a slave, chained to the galleys. I have tried, but nothing has happened. If I am a slave, why not slump at my oars like a slave?"

But Ben Hur was patient, and life rewarded his patience with a magnificent outpouring of rich gifts. You know the story. The shipwreck. The rescue of the tribune. The glory and the happiness, made keen by contrast with the misery. The chariot race. The laurel wreath.

IV

The Courage to Meet Life's Daily Tests

The things that batter down morale and send us home at night feeling that we can never again pick up the load are not big things but little things, not grave emergencies but insignificant irritations. A thousand and one petty disturbances gnaw at our patience, upset our poise, work us into a state of nervous instability, until we feel as if we could no longer stand the strain. These little things stretch us on the rack until the cord of poise and patience breaks.

Clay W. Hamlin, whose life is a romance of courage, once was a meek, half-frightened little salesman—a failure if there ever was one. Three times he tried to make a living selling, and three times he failed. In and out of offices he would go, timid, scared, ineffective. Three times general agents advised him to quit, and three times he did quit.

> *But with a determination that braver and bigger men might have lacked, he came back a fourth time, doggedly sure that this time he would not quit. Within a year Clay*

> *Hamlin had written over $250,000 insurance, which was a production higher than that of the average agent in those years. The second year he raised his volume to more than $750,000. And the third year his "paid-for" went soaring above the million mark.*

Clay Hamlin! Little, meek, half-frightened! He is still little and, one would say, mild, but today he ranks as one of the greatest salesmen the life insurance business has ever developed.

"We don't need the courage to face life's big tests," says Mr. Hamlin. "What we need is the courage to meet life's little tests. What we need is the courage to follow a regular routine, the courage to stick to our plans, the courage to keep the petty irritations of the day from blocking our efforts, the courage to keep on going hour after hour. We need to remember that it isn't the big trees that trip us up as we walk through the forest, but the vines on the ground, the exposed roots, the low under-brush."

This is a different kind of courage from that which sends the soldier across the fields into a burst of flame, different from the courage that sends the beach patrol into the thundering surf of a winter's storm, different from the courage that endures one great moment of exertion and of risk, different but none the less as great. For it is the courage that keeps a man sweet in the daily grind, casting off petty irritations, overlooking fancied insults, meeting irksome details with a smile and a mind undisturbed.

One of the greatest gifts you can give yourself is the courage to master life's daily tests!

V

The Courage to Keep Your Mind Free From Worry

God broke the endless circle of time into hours and days so that, hour by hour and day by day, we might be able to go along and keep quite strong. But we in our foolishness act as if we were wiser than God. We take all the weight of worry and strife which we believe we will meet in the future and carry it now, instead of allowing it to rest in peace until the time comes for it to trouble us.

We forget that there is a lifetime ahead in which to solve the problems that will be met. The fact that life's experience teaches us that future problems must someday be solved does not mean that we must begin their solution today. We have a lifetime in which to solve them, and all that is asked of us is that we solve today's problems today. Tomorrow's problems will come, but time enough to solve tomorrow's problems tomorrow.

Sufficient unto the day is the evil thereof.

Build in your mind worry-proof compartments, and then live each day in one compartment, shut off from yesterday, untroubled by tomorrow, making the most of each day's opportunities. This is not the imprudent doctrine of indifference, or carelessness, or delayed thinking. Rather it is the doctrine of a man free to give to each day's problems the best that is in him.

The way to free the mind from worry today is to do something about today's problems today. Inaction and not action makes men snap under the load. Worry about money, worry about business, worry about the family, worry about health, worry about the job—worry isn't the way to solve these problems. Do something about each problem.

Money matters? Do something about them! Notes due at the bank? IOU's falling due? Unpaid current bills? Put these items in the budget, and arrange to pay them month by month. Make the adjustments necessary in your living standards. Get your financial house in order. Do something. Health? Go down to the doctor and tell him to get busy with his stethoscope. Throw the responsibility on him. Do something. Worrying won't help.

Your job! If you are unhappy, do something about it. Lay out your plans. Get a vision of what you could do if you would do all that you could do and all that you want to do. Determine what you want to do, and then do the things necessary to do it. Do something about your job. Don't stew and fret about it. Don't go on day after day doing the unpleasant, irksome, unhappy work. Keep your goal before your eyes. Turn every moment of your day into a step toward that goal. Do something definite about it.

Live each day in a worry-proof compartment. Refuse to worry about the future, and give yourself a basis for that attitude by substituting action for worry and by doing something about the problems that press most heavily.

VI

The Courage that Comes From Constructive Thinking

Hang on the walls of your mind the memory of your successes. Give yourself the courage to stand at the door of your mind like a stern watchman who, sword in hand, bars the way to all thoughts of failure, all thoughts that are negative, all thoughts that tend to tear down instead of build up, all thoughts that will make you a poorer man.

"Shut up a man in a dark room," someone has said, "and in ten years he will be blind. If you shut up your mind in a dark room, a room filled with dark pictures of past failures, then you become blind to everything excepting failure."

For your mind is a closed room in which you live all of your life. You walk about in this closed room day after day and year after year. On its walls you hang pictures at which you look day after day, year after year.

Pace your narrow cell, oh prisoner, all the years of your life, with the pictures you have hung before you! What happens? Inevitably you become like the pictures at which you look. It is a law from which you cannot escape.

Why then hang in your mind pictures of failure, of lack of self-confidence, of weakness, of fear? Why not, instead, hang the pictures of the best things that you have ever done, the best things that men like you have done? Why spend a lifetime looking at the negative, the uninspiring, the dark and the fearful? Will that make for success?

In his youth, Harry Lauder sang in beer parlors for little more than a bite to eat and a few shillings. Then Lauder determined to master one song so completely that with it he could move men's emotions. He selected the old Scotch refrain, *"Roamin' in the Gloamin',"* and for two long years Lauder sang it over and over again. He studied every lilt in the refrain; he studied every phrase; he rehearsed it, so he tells us, not less than 10,000 times. Then he assembled 120 different combinations of Scotch garb before finally finding exactly the right combination. Then he went upon the concert stage and sang *"Roamin' in the Gloamin',"* and it brought him knighthood. Upon that single success, Lauder went on to fame and fortune! So it is with you. Upon a single success you, too, can build a career all men will envy!

Hang on the walls of your mind the memory of your successes. Take counsel of your strength, not your weakness. Think of the good jobs you have done. Think of the times when you rose above your average level of performance and carried out an idea, or a dream, or a desire for which you had deeply longed.

Think of the big moments in your life! Hang those pictures on the walls of your mind, and look at them as you travel the roadway of life.

VII

The Courage to Utilize Your Full Potential

You remember the old fifth reader story of the lion cub that strayed into a flock of sheep, grew up with the sheep, ran and played with them, and behaved as if he were a sheep. Then one day on the distant skyline the silhouette of a lion appeared, head thrown back, tail lashing about. With a great roar, the lion on the hillside sent his voice across the fields, and the lion playing with the sheep stopped his playing. Something stirred within him. Like called to like. He knew then that he was a lion and not a sheep, and with an answering roar that sent the timid sheep scattering before him, the lion with the sheep ran to join the lion on the hillside.

We go on and on with the lion asleep within us, never realizing that our lot in life is not in the meadows with the sheep, but that it is on the hillside with the lions.

We never make an earnest attempt to arouse and to utilize the potential power within. We are satisfied to measure ourselves against other men, our record against their records.

> We live under the curse of too much deadening conversation about the average man, forgetting that the man who is only average is as close to the bottom as he is to the top, like Christopher Robin on the stairs, half-way up and half-way down.

As we grow older, we stop measuring ourselves by our own ambitions. We begin, instead, to measure ourselves by what other men are doing. The average! The average man drives such-and-such a car, we are told. The average man earns so much money every year. The average man spends so much on groceries. The average man has a two-week vacation every year.

Once upon a time when a middle-aged man was clearing the rubbish out of an attic, he discovered an old notebook he had kept as a boy. There it was, its pages discolored by years of attic dust, but bearing the plans he had set down so many years ago for himself. Great things to be done, definite ways for doing them. A life that would count. A name with which to reckon. The man sat down on the stairs and slowly read each page, without the heart to throw the notebook away, for it was the biography of the man he meant to be, of the man he might have been. Why didn't youth's dreams become accomplishments in later years? Because he measured his efforts and rewards by those of other men.

> Across the fields of yesterday, he sometimes comes to me: a little lad just back from play,

the lad I used to be. And yet he smiles so wistfully, once he has crept within, I wonder if he hopes to see the man I might have been.

The ability to dream of great achievements was not given us to mock us. The fact that once we were inspired to believe that the high road was the right road is evidence that we possess the ability to climb that road.

Bring back those old dreams of hoped-for achievement, and place them once more in command! Then through planned activity call out the force of potential power, and make your dreams come true.

> *Though everything looks dark and drear, I shall succeed. Though failure's voice speaks in my ear, I shall succeed. I do not fear misfortune's blow. I tower with strength above each foe. I stand erect because I know I shall succeed. Night swoops on me with darkest wings, but I'll succeed. I see the stars that darkness brings, but I'll succeed. No force on earth shall make me cower, because each moment and each hour, I still affirm with strength and power: I shall succeed.*

Give yourself the courage to utilize your full potential—to live up to what you know you can do!

VIII

The Courage to Meet Mental Depressions

Give yourself the courage to meet the valley days when they come. Just as the business line is a series of sharp hills and valleys, so is the map of a man's attitude and state of mind. We have learned that the cycles in the business chart are a part of a program, a swing of the pendulum that is inherent in life and in its affairs. The ups and downs in a man's state of mind likewise are a part of the scheme of things.

For life is not a walk along a level roadway, but a long journey over hills and valleys, and the valleys are as much a part of the journey as are the hilltops. Take away the valleys, and there would be no hills.

> *We have hilltop days and valley days, and the trick in life is not to be discouraged when valley days come, not to be surprised when they come, not to be alarmed, not to believe that all of life ahead is to be a valley day.*

Perhaps yesterday was fine, a hilltop day. You were on top of the world, and your heart sang to the glory of the hilltops and the fair prospect of the roadway ahead. The colors in life's pattern were brilliant. Nature sang too as you went to work, and the elements of the universe tuned in with the rhythm of your soul. The whole world stood at attention and saluted when you passed. You were a conqueror marching through triumphal arches, taking cities, commanding men. A hilltop day!

But today! Well, today is different. Today is a valley day. You can't click. Your brain has lost its cunning. Your tongue stammers. The old inferiority complex captures the throne of reason. You are awkward and clumsy. Your vision is gone. Your self-confidence is gone. The future looks dark, and you approach the day's task with a little sigh of self-pity.

The calm of your existence may seem to be shattered, but fundamentally nothing is wrong.

> *Perhaps this morning you broke a shoestring. Perhaps you spoke grumpily to an acquaintance, and the response you received was about as cheerful as a bulldog's snarl. Perhaps your toast was burned. Perhaps your stenographer was late. Perhaps you got your feet wet, or the stock market didn't show the rise you expected. Perhaps you have lost some money. Perhaps the details of your business are in a frightful tangle.*

Perhaps—oh, a thousand things may have gone wrong with you, one after another, until you believe that each successive one is worse than its predecessor. The day may start with so small a thing as a broken shoestring, or a torn button on a shirt, or a rip in a sock when one is late, and unless we watch ourselves, it colors our whole day. We lose our perspective. We blindly believe, in our overwhelming pessimism, that the things of today will last forever—today's thoughts, today's disappointments, today's problems, today's unhappiness.

Never forget that discouragement is a part of the plan, and that if we will only take to the road fearlessly, walk on, one step and then another, so hilltop will follow valley as surely as day follows night.

IX

The Courage of a Dogged Determination

Give yourself the courage of a dogged determination. Be brave. Be as brave as was the small boy who awakened night after night screaming because of a repeated dream in which he met a tiger. His mental condition was affected by this nightly terror, and so his parents counseled with a physician who said to him: "The next time you dream about that tiger say to yourself:

> *This old fellow hasn't come to hurt me. He's a friendly old chap. I'm going to walk right up and pat him on the head."*

The boy agreed and that night the anxious parents stole into his room. There he lay tossing nervously in his sleep. Then they saw his face whiten, his breath shorten, and through tightly closed lips father and mother heard a desperate little voice say, "I'm not afraid! I'm not afraid! I'm going to walk right up to that tiger and pat him on the head." Then the boy smiled in his sleep, and the parents knew that the tiger would never again send him screaming from his bed.

> *This is the courage to give yourself, the courage to say to the tigers you meet, the fears and troubles and discouragements that are a part of life, I'm not afraid of you. You haven't come to hurt me. You have come to test my courage. You are a part of life.*

Give yourself the courage of a determination that counts, a determination that is greater than chance or destiny or fate, a determination so great that earnest purpose never swerves.

X

The Kind of Courage Needed

Give yourself the courage that strengthened the heart of Columbus when he sailed head-on into the hazards of the unknown seas, the courage that held him steadfast to his westward course through dark days and stormy nights, the courage that enabled him day after day to greet his fear-stricken sailors with the cry, "Sail on! Sail on!"

Give yourself the courage that sustained the great heart of Washington during the dark days at Valley Forge, when the flickering camp fires of his band of ragged soldiers lit up the starless nights. Dissension within, disloyalty without, the menacing gales of winter, and yet withal the great commander hung on grimly.

Give yourself the courage that sent John Brown singing to the gallows, his path to death lighted by his vision of a nation growing into greatness through the years ahead.

Give yourself the courage that supported the immortal Lincoln during four long years of national agony.

Give yourself the courage that led Henley to sing victoriously:

> *It matters not how strait the gate,*
> *How charged with punishment the scroll,*
> *I am the master of my fate,*
> *I am the captain of my soul.*

Where was Henley when he sang these brave words? Healthy? Prosperous? Riding the crest of the wave? Rich in friends? No. Henley was friendless. He was poor. He was a charity patient in a hospital in Edinburgh while surgeons battled to snatch him back from death's doors. What were the sounds that came from the grim old walls of Lister's hospital? What were the words he wrote from his bed?

> *I am master of my fate,*
> *I am the captain of my soul.*

Give yourself the courage that kept Hugo Anderson playing as a substitute on Northwestern University's football team for three long years, letting the varsity batter him week after week, never making the team, but never quitting. This same Hugo Anderson, failing to make the grade in an officers' training camp, went on to France as a private, never quitting. In Flanders, he saw a wounded companion in the line of fire. He went over the top, pulled the wounded soldier safely back to the trench, and fell dead from a machine gun bullet—never quitting.

Give yourself the courage that led Captain Scott on his ill-fated Antarctic Expedition to write this note:

> *We are pegging out in a very comfortless spot. Hoping this letter may be found and sent to you, I write you a word of farewell. I want you to think well of me and of my end.*

Goodbye. I am not at all afraid of the end, but sad to miss many a simple pleasure that I had planned for the future on our long marches.

We are in a desperate state—feet frozen, no fuel and a long way from food. But it would do your heart good to be in our tent, to hear our songs and cheery conversation.

We are very near the end.

Stand for a moment by that dark tent, lost in the dreary wastes of an Antarctic wilderness, blackness overhead, blackness all around, but no blackness in the hearts of Scott and his men. Listen to the cheery conversation and the songs of men doomed to die.

Give yourself the courage of Dr. Brooks of Baylor University. The 67-year-old president lay dying of cancer. His massive frame was gutted. Death sat at his bedside watching him sign the diplomas of the graduating class. First a hundred a day. Then forty. Then ten, and as the pen dropped from his hand, he whispered: "I have tried to teach these boys and girls how to live. Now I wish to teach them how to die!"

Give yourself the courage of Francis Parkman, the historian. His eyes were so weak he could not write his own name except by closing them. Every effort cost him great pain. Yet by using a wooden frame, across which wires were stretched to correspond to the lines on a sheet of paper, he could close his eyes and write. In this slow and painful way, Parkman wrote eight great histories of the Indian wars, books which to this day are standard reference histories.

Give yourself the courage of the boy who paid his way through college by working from two o'clock each morning until eight, tending the ovens in a bakery. From seven to nine each night he waited on customers. The rest of the day and night he went to classes and studied. In three years he had saved enough so that in his last year he could live like the other fellows. His roommate became seriously ill. Money was needed for an operation. So this nameless hero, one of the bravest men who ever lived, drew his savings from the bank, paid for his chum's operation and went back to work in the bakery.

Give yourself the courage of Lazear and Carroll and Folk and Cooke and Jernegan. The scene, Cuba. The state of affairs, bad. Old Man Yellow Jack was running amuck and was killing thousands. Perhaps the sting of a mosquito was causing the epidemic. Scientists thought so. No one was sure. Humans were needed for the experiment to determine how the disease was spreading. So Lazear and Carroll and Folk and Cooke and Jernegan offered themselves to the doctors. Into a little house they went. They sat on the edge of their army cots and watched the little silver-striped mosquitoes settle silently on their arms. Then they lay down to fight through the Valley of the Shadow, in order that Old Man Yellow Jack might forever be vanquished.

Stand for a moment outside that crude little house in the army camp in Cuba, and reflect upon the bravery of the men within.

Give yourself the courage of John M. Siddall, one-time editor of the *American Magazine*. The doctors told him that an insidious disease was at work and that death was only a matter of a few weeks or a few months. Siddall asked the doctors to keep their secret, telling them that he proposed to meet death like a soldier at his post. So he went about his work with a cheery smile as if all were well with him and with his world. Siddall was interested only in victory. He won it. Give yourself that kind of courage.

What a glorious gallery of pictures is this! Humanity at its best! Man at his noblest! The very essence of courage, sublime in its greatness!

The Priceless Jewel

Take courage as your companion through all the days ahead, the same companion that the noble men and women of all ages have had as their closest friend—the courage to act now, the courage to keep on trying, the courage to master life's daily irksome tasks, the courage to keep one's mind free from worry, the courage to bar all negative thoughts, the courage to live up to our full potentials, the courage to know that success will come, the courage to meet the valley days, the courage of a dogged determination, the courage to eliminate fear by determining to win.

Give yourself the courage to build a philosophy of life under which you can live as a new man in a new world, finding kinship with kings who conquer. Force yourself into the banquet hall of life, and take your place at the table of leaders!

Like Captain Scott and his men, peg away in your comfortless spot. Perhaps you are lonely, disappointed, suffering privations from the day's long tramp, but keep aglow a heart warmed by cheery songs and a vision of the goal-star shining somewhere in the long, black night.

> *That is courage, the priceless jewel which you can give yourself but that no one else can give you!*

Recommended Reading

If you have enjoyed reading this book, perhaps you will also enjoy any or all of the following publications.

Christenson, Kathryn and Miller, Kevin, editors. *Tributes To Courage.* This book highlights the lives of thirteen people who have overcome severe physical disabilities and become useful, productive members of society. Golden Valley, MN: Courage Center, 1980, a rehabilitation organization. 144 pp.

Considine, Bob. *They Rose Above It.* True stories about men, women, and children who fought back in the face of pain, doubt and dismay—people who looked inside themselves and found the strength and courage to go on in the face of adversity and terrible odds. New York: Doubleday and Company, 1977. 111 pp.

Gaddis, Vincent H. *Courage in Crisis.* Dramatic tales of heroism in the face of danger include a woman who had to instantly learn how to fly their two-seater plane when her pilot-husband died, a bus driver's 12-mile trek through a blizzard to help his stranded passengers, and a maintenance worker's halt of a runaway diesel train. New York: Hawthorn Books, Inc. 1973. 184 pp.

Heinz, W. C. *American Mirror.* A distinguished writer portrays ordinary people who performed with courage under pressure in extreme situations. This book includes the sports world and some World War I spies who were shot. New York: Doubleday and Company, 1982. 256 pp.

Kennedy, John F. *Profiles in Courage.* Written by the 35th President of the United States, this book won the 1957 Pulitzer Prize Award. It tells the tale of many courageous American historical figures. New York: Harper and Row. 1955. 266 pp.

Recommended Reading (Continued)

Lash, Joseph P. *Helen and Teacher.* The story of Helen Keller, deaf-mute-blind and her teacher, Anne Sullivan Macy, is intensely interesting and inspirational. New York: Delacorte Press, 1980.

Parker, William, editor. *Men of Courage.* True stories of present-day adventures in the face of danger and death. Twenty gripping stories of real-life adventure that range from mountain climbing to undersea exploration, from successful island escape to death in the bullfight arena. The chapter entitled, "Bloody Road to Usumbura" is reason enough to search out this book. Chicago: Playboy Press Book, 1972. 268 pp.

Moses, John B., M.D. and Cross, Wilbur. *Presidential Courage.* The dramatic and fascinating stories of American presidents confronted by the combined challenges of very poor health and political crises. New York: W. W. Norton and Company, 1980. 249 pp.

Rivera, Geraldo. *A Special Kind of Courage.* Profiles of eleven heroic young Americans who acted with bravery and honor at moments of individual crisis, including well-known Edward Kennedy, Jr., who learned to live a normal life despite a permanently crippling disease and movie subject Joey Cappelletti, who set an example of quiet valor in his day-to-day struggle against leukemia. New York: Simon and Schuster, 1976. 319 pp.

Index

Achievement, 17
Anderson, Hugo, 26
Averageness, 16
Brooks, Samuel Palmer, 27
Brown, John, 25
Carroll, James, 28
Columbus, Christopher, 25
Constructive thinking, 13-14
Cooke, Robert P., 28
Courage;
    defined, 1-2
    of constructive thinking, 13-14
    of determination, 23-24
    of fifteen famous men, 25-29
    of persistence, 5-6
    to keep free from worry, 11-12
    to meet daily irritations, 9-10
    to meet depression, 19-21
    to not procrastinate, 3-4
    to use your full potential, 15-17
    rewards of, 7-8
Depression, 19-21
Determination, 23-24
Folk, Levi E., 28
Hamlin, Clay W., 9-10
Henley, William Ernest, 25-26
Henry, O. (a.k.a. William Sidney Porter), 3-4
Inaction, 12
Irritations, 9-10
Jernegan, Warren G., 28
Job, Book of, 12
Lauder, Harry, 13
Lazear, Jesse William, 28
Lincoln, Abraham, 25
Money, 12
O. Henry (see Henry, O.)
Parkman, Francis, 27-28
Patience, 7-8
Persistence, 5-6
Potential, 15-16
Procrastination, 3-4
Rewards, 7-8
Scott, Robert Falcon, 26-27, 31
Self-confidence, 2
Siddall, John M., 29
Tarkington, Booth, 5-6
Washington, George, 25
Worry, 11-12

About the Author
1893-1952

The late Paul Speicher received his early education in Northern Ohio and later graduated from the University of Wisconsin with an M.A. Degree. After teaching for several years, he turned his educational talents to the life insurance field. He became an editor with the Insurance Research & Review Service, Inc. in 1922, subsequently being appointed managing editor in 1934. Three years later he was named president of the company, a position he held for fifteen years. His thousands of friends and admirers described him as "a man of vision" and "a master-friend and a master-workman."

Speicher was a noted pioneer in producing organized sales training courses for life insurance agents and wrote numerous articles concerning the principles of life insurance selling. He was widely acclaimed as a speaker, for he spoke from the platform with the same deep-rooted conviction which characterized his many writings. Speicher died in 1952 at the age of 59 following a brief illness.

Hugh P. O'Kane

In 1960, early in the history of this book, *The Gift of Courage*, Hugh O'Kane was given a copy. At that time he was an insurance salesman. Over the next three decades, he used it for personal motivation in his sales career, often giving copies to friends. Through the years O'Kane struggled, succeeded, failed and struggled again as he strove to support his family of eight children through his chosen career in selling. After reading *The Gift of Courage* he took to heart the chapter entitled "The Courage to Keep On Trying" and eventually he became proficient at the fine art of selling.

When O'Kane discovered that *The Gift of Courage* had gone out of print, he encouraged Diction Books to obtain the rights and reprint this valuable, inspirational book.

O'Kane has been with Juran and Moody, a municipal bond house, for nearly two decades and is currently a vice president and senior partner with the firm. In a company with over fifty salesmen, he has been one of the top producers year after year. O'Kane was raised on a farm in southern Minnesota and he and his family now reside in North Oaks, Minnesota. Hugh P. O'Kane, an eloquent baritone speaker, shares *The Gift of Courage* with audiences of all types.

To obtain additional copies of this book or to engage Hugh P. O'Kane as a speaker, contact Diction Books, 1313 Fifth Street S.E., Suite 104B, Minneapolis, MN 55414, (612) 623-9533.